MATT MAHER
EMPTY & BEAUTIFUL

EDITOR: Andrew High
TRANSCRIBER: Paul Nelson
COVER ADAPTATION: Susannah Parrish
PRODUCTION COORDINATOR: Liz George
EXECUTIVE PRODUCER: John J. Thompson

WORSHIP TOGETHER.com®   essential   SONY BMG MUSIC ENTERTAINMENT

MATT MAHER
EMPTY & BEAUTIFUL
TABLE OF CONTENTS

Your Grace Is Enough

Words and Music by
MATT MAHER

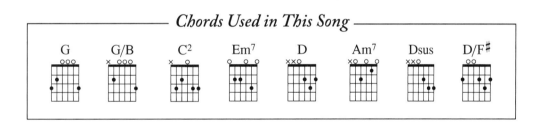

Chords Used in This Song

This page has been left intentionally blank to avoid awkward page turns.

Look Like a Fool

Words and Music by
MATT MAHER and
BILL STAINES

VERSE 1

1. All God's crea-tures got a place in the choir: ___

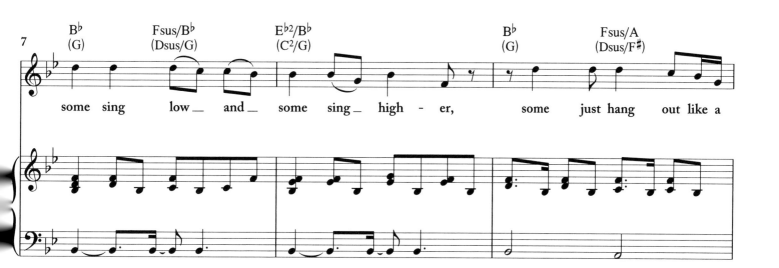

some sing low ___ and ___ some sing ___ high - er, some just hang out like a

16

Chords Used in This Song

For Your Glory

Words and Music by
MATT MAHER

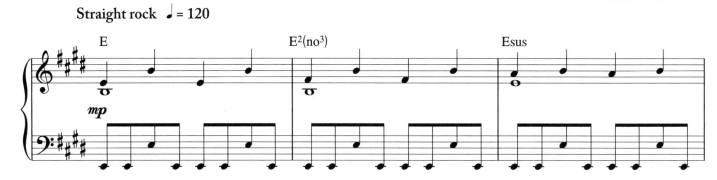

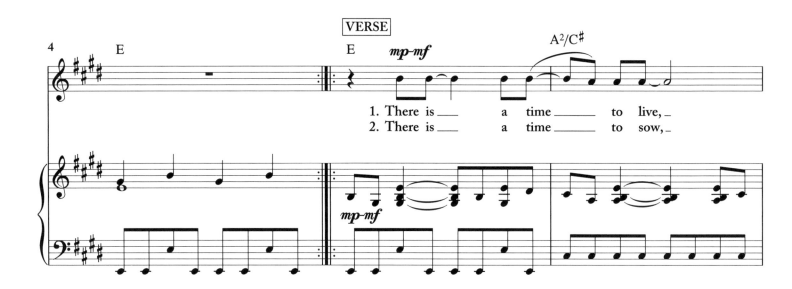

1. There is ___ a time ___ to live, ___
2. There is ___ a time ___ to sow, ___

there is ___ a time ___ to die, ___   there is ___ a time ___
there is ___ a time ___ to reap, ___   a time ___ for vic -

Chords Used in This Song

As It Is in Heaven

Words and Music by
MATT MAHER
and ED CASH

34

Chords Used in This Song

I Rejoice

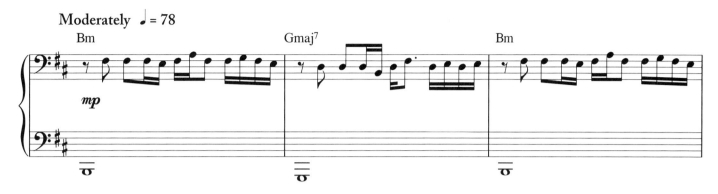

Words and Music by
MATT MAHER

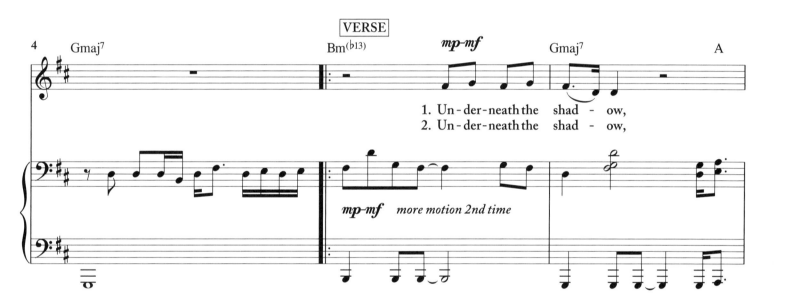

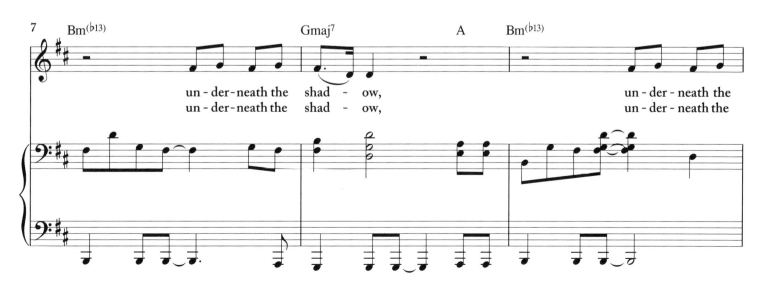

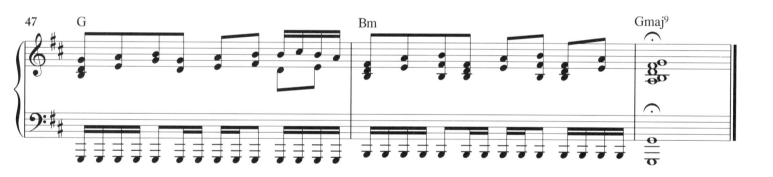

Chords Used in This Song

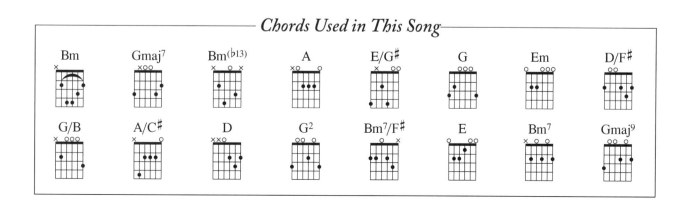

Maranatha (Come Again)

Words and Music by
MATT MAHER

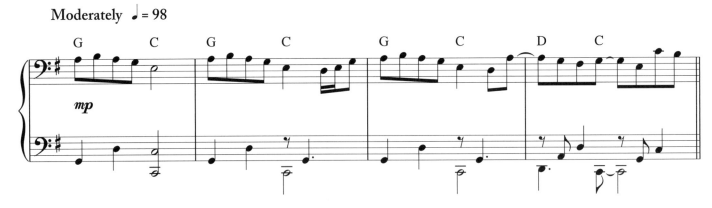

1. Come, let us go to the house of the Lord, the King-
2. And now we see as in a mir-ror re-flec-

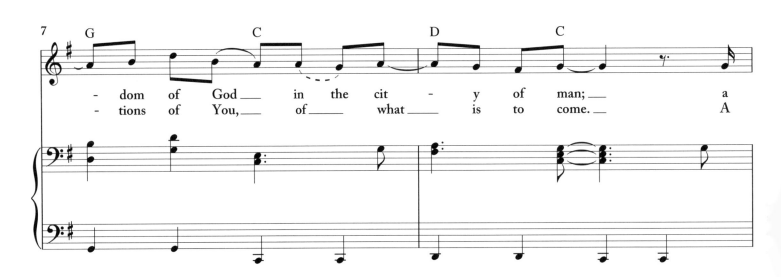

-dom of God in the cit-y of man; a
-tions of You, of what is to come. A

Chords Used in This Song

Great Things

Words and Music by
MATT MAHER

With a strong backbeat ♩ = 136

VERSE

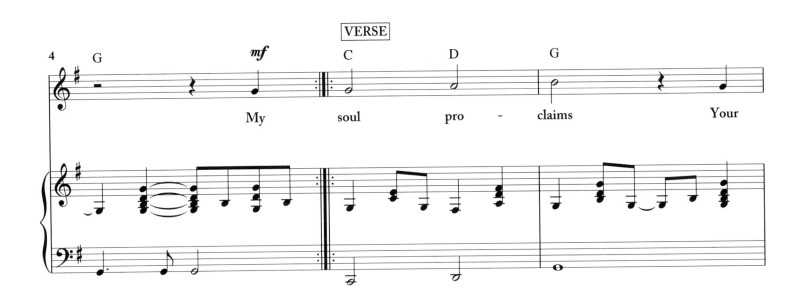

My soul pro - claims Your

great - ness, Lord, re - joic - ing

48

CHORUS

done great things, __ I can't boast of an - y - thing; __

Mighty One, and King of kings, __ Je - sus. __

You a - lone have done great things __

by Your liv - ing word in me; __ Might - y One, and

shout - ing out loud. It's Your name we're shout - ing out,

shout - ing out.

Chords Used in This Song

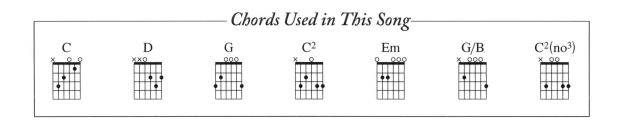

Leave a Light On

Words and Music by
MATT MAHER

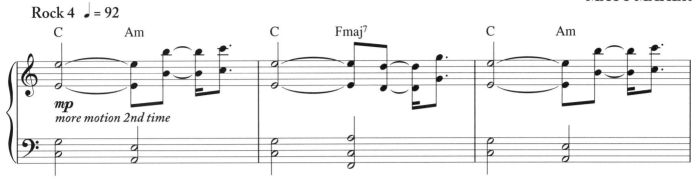

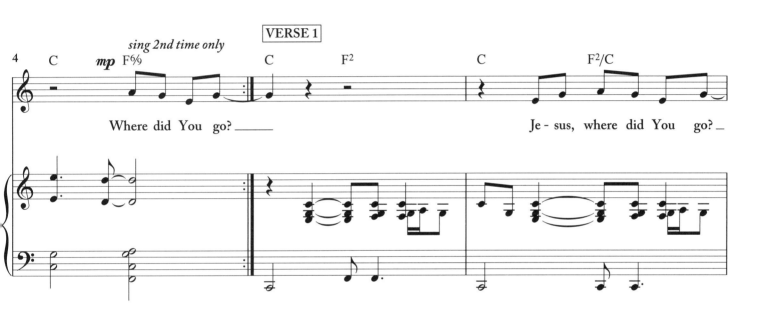

Where did You go? _____

Je - sus, where did You go? _

You flew in - to the clouds, _

we wor-ship and we doubt; _

Chords Used in This Song

Shine Like the Son

Words and Music by
MATT MAHER

With energy! ♩ = 150

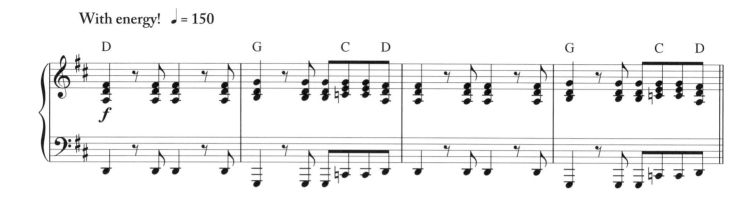

VERSE

1. How beau-ti-ful are the hands and feet of
2. How beau-ti-ful are the hands and feet of

those bring-ing the good news to all the world, bring-ing the good
those work-ing in the vine-yard of the Lord, work-ing in the

BRIDGE

Unwavering

Words and Music by
MATT MAHER

Capo 3 (C)

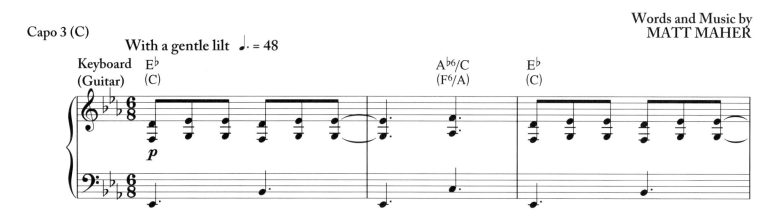

VERSE 1

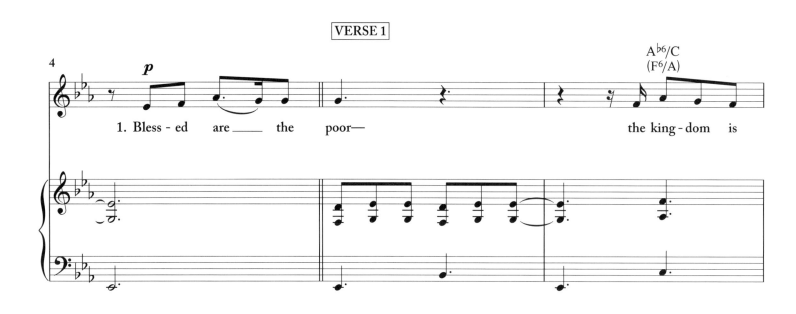

1. Bless - ed are ___ the poor— the king-dom is

theirs, a - live in the prom - ise

This page has been left intentionally blank to avoid awkward page turns.

Lay It Down

Words and Music by
MATT MAHER and
BRENTON BROWN

Empty and Beautiful

Capo 1 (G)

Gently and freely ♩ = 76

Words and Music by
MATT MAHER

the faith in me.

Chords Used in This Song

YOUR GRACE IS ENOUGH

This is probably the oldest song on the record, and I'm thankful so many people have appreciated it. I wrote it when I was going through some hard times in my life. I found myself on the back patio at home with my guitar, reading the Psalms, and I kept singing the same word: "Remember. Remember. Remember…" In the Psalms, David is crying out to God to remember His people. I was fascinated by that and began writing this song I was calling "Remember," asking God to remember us as we remember Him. When we recall the language of God's covenant, we end up being in a space where God is already remembering us. The chorus came from Paul's letter to the Romans, and the idea of the thorn in Paul's side, begging God to take it away. I think in my mid-twenties, the thorn in my side was loneliness; I was like, "OK God, give me something to fill that space." I think God comes to us and says, "No, I need to be enough."

LOOK LIKE A FOOL

The whole premise of Christianity is foolishness to the world. The things we do – feeding the hungry, clothing the naked—those are the fruits of a good prayer life. Christianity itself is completely counter-cultural. Put all that together, and the song becomes the expression of "I don't care if I look foolish to the world." This is what God calls us to do. (1 Corinthians 1:18)

FOR YOUR GLORY

The writer of Ecclesiastes says there's nothing new under the sun; that there's nothing we can think of that God hasn't already thought of, and that there's an appointed time for everything in life. So how do you respond to that actively? Do you just throw up your arms? Well, yes. As a Christian, you have the opportunity in every situation to experience the passion, death and resurrection of Jesus. Everything becomes an opportunity to give glory to God – our laughing and our crying; our dancing and our mourning. Whatever it is, we can give glory to God.

AS IT IS IN HEAVEN

I wrote this one in the fall of 2004, after I hadn't written anything in months. I was originally thinking about the sufficiency of God as the Father of all; that's the "new song" sung about in Psalm 40. Fast forward three years. The record was done, but I felt like something was missing. My A&R director, Blaine Barcus, suggested that I work on it with Ed Cash. Ed heard the song and fell in love with the pre-chorus and chorus. We decided to break open the Lord's Prayer, which was where the chorus came from. The verses came out in 15 minutes over iChat. We both knew God's hand was moving. The whole process of rewriting and rerecording this song was a testament to unity; and I hope that this song becomes a way for people of all denominations to come together, and say that God is Father of all.

I REJOICE

"Underneath the shadow of Your wings, I rejoice in You" – that was all I had for the longest time. I'd started crafting musical ideas and layering them on Garage Band on my computer, with only those words. A year later I was praying, singing, "I rejoice, I rejoice, I rejoice," and I asked myself, "What am I rejoicing in?" I realized I was rejoicing in God, and I just want to sing it! Then I had a conversation about the image of the Shadow of God's wings, and I thought of the shadow of Jesus' arms on the cross – we are in the shadow of the cross, filled with the light of the resurrection. There we rejoice in our adoption as God's children.

MARANATHA (COME AGAIN)

"Maranatha," or "Come Again," started primarily as an instrumental, musical idea. I had these lyrics for a really long time, based on Psalm 122, lyrics that pertained to the idea of going up to the House of the Lord. However, the Lord came here. I started to ask "what kind of impact does that idea have on the psalmist…what does that portray in regards to the orphans and widows?" In my mind, it portrays how the lowest of low are being made great in the kingdom. The chorus was originally a bridge because I wanted the bridge to be about Christ returning as the House of God on earth. That's where the idea of "Maranatha," or "Come Again" came from…taking the imagery of Christ coming, of Him feeding His flock – and using us in the process to portray that – i.e., we are the 'cloud of witnesses,' like what Paul talks about when he describes those who have been marginalized - responded to the call of following Christ.

GREAT THINGS

One day I was looking again at the Magnificat, Mary's prayer at Jesus' birth announcement, and I thought of it as the first prayer ever prayed by somebody saying yes to the will of God. Some weeks later, I was practicing with my band and realized what I wanted was to combine Paul's foundational theology with the theology of the incarnation: "You alone have done great things/ I can't boast of anything/ Mighty one, King of kings, Jesus/ You alone have done great things by Your living word in me." The idea was to echo that what happened to Mary, happens to us as Christians. When we say yes to God, we receive the Word into us. Mary's situation happened in a very, very unique and profound way. As Christians, we can have a similar spiritual encounter.

Funny side-note: As the production took off, it became more and more like a country song! Every one was like, "You wrote a country song!" Well, I didn't really mean it to be; it just kind of went that way.

LEAVE A LIGHT ON

For the record, I had no idea that "We'll leave the light on" was Motel 6's tagline. I grew up in Canada! I had not a clue. I had heard a talk on Pentecost, and how at the Ascension, there was the reality of worshipping in the presence of God, but doubt still existed. There's comfort in that. We watch the glory of God make itself known and manifest in the world one second, and strain to see Him in our own hearts the next. Herein lies the call to faithfulness. Jesus used the parable of 10 virgins with lamp stands; that some ran out of oil...that His coming would be sudden...to keep watch and be ready...so as I worship and doubt, I'll leave a light on. That light is the fire of His own Spirit, once again affirming that I cannot do it on my own; I need Him in me to stay ready.

SHINE LIKE THE SON

It's relatively simple; the song is breaking open the familiar words, "How beautiful is the sound of those who bring good news." God made us ready to shine like the sun. Well, there was some confusion, and a long story short, I eventually decided to change sun to Son. But the point is this: We are called to live in the middle of the lost and the poor. There is a tendency, especially sometimes in American, Christian culture, to construct a very safe environment to live in—to the point where we don't know anybody who's been marginalized. I think we are called to be salt and light. We are called to go into the middle of where people are, just as God comes into the middle of wherever we are.

UNWAVERING

I have friends who were forced to leave New Orleans because of Hurricane Katrina. Overnight, my best friend, Paul George, went from doing a simple Bible study to building showers everyday, and helping grown men get clothing. My friend was a school teacher in New Orleans, and she lost everything. I remember looking on TV at images of the poor—it was like they had come out of nowhere. This song came from watching all of this poverty unfold, and yet sensing God's unwavering plan. We are sent out to be God's hands and feet, and the neat thing about being in solidarity with the poor, is that when you are poor, you are completely dead to the world. It doesn't really have much control over you, because you recognize your own poverty. We all need Jesus.

LAY IT DOWN

The verse and the chorus came, as many of my songs do, in the midst of a worship time. Someone was talking about laying all of our stuff down at the feet of Jesus, and I started singing, "Everything I am/ Everything I long to be/ I'll lay it down at Your feet." I believe I wrote that in the fall of 2003, or earlier, and had it for a long time. Then, in the spring of 2006, Brenton Brown and I got together to write. We talked about how amazing it is that what we lay down is so minuscule compared to what God gives us. Yet, beautiful surrender happens, and brings us closer to God.

EMPTY AND BEAUTIFUL

For me as a Christian, I'm realizing more and more that the world isn't my worst enemy—I'm my biggest enemy. If I could spend more time letting God love me, then maybe I'd be a more effective apostle. That's why we can look at a cross and not see death, but rather the grace of love, forgiveness and hope. The chorus was inspired by Second Timothy: "I fought the fight, I've kept the faith, I've finished the race." I believe Paul's not saying that as a boasting man; he'd been abandoned and rejected, scorned and lost. But Paul knows grace. He knows the biggest battle he's fought is not against the world, but against his self.

Your Grace Is Enough

MATT MAHER and CHRIS TOMLIN

KEY OF (A)

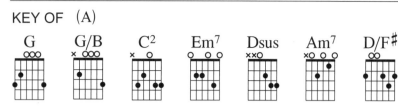

G   G/B   C² Em⁷   Dsus   Am⁷   D/F♯

capo 2nd fret (G) VERSE 1:

G   G/B   C²
   Great is Your faithfulness, oh God

Em⁷   Dsus   C²
   You wrestle with   the sinner's heart

G   G/B   C²
   You lead us by   still waters into mercy

Em⁷   Dsus   C²
   And nothing can   keep us apart

CHANNEL:

   Am⁷   G/B   C²   Dsus
So remember Your people, remember Your children

Em⁷   G   C²
Remember Your promise, oh God

CHORUS:

   G   Dsus   Em⁷   C²
Your grace is enough,   Your grace is enough

   G   Dsus   C²
Your grace is enough   for me

VERSE 2:

G   G/B   C²
  Great is Your love   and justice, God

Em⁷   Dsus   C²
   You use the weak   to lead the strong

G   G/B   C²
   You lead us in   the song of Your   salvation

Em⁷   Dsus   C²
   And all Your people sing along

(Repeat CHANNEL and CHORUS)

(Repeat CHORUS)

CHANNEL 2:

   Am⁷   G/B   C²   Dsus
So remember Your people, remember Your children

   Em⁷   D/F♯   G   C²
Remember Your promise,   oh God

CONTINUED...

CHORUS 2:

   G   Dsus
Your grace is enough

          Em⁷   C²
Heaven reaching down to us

          G   Dsus
God I see Your grace is enough

    Em⁷   C²
I'm covered in Your love

   G   Dsus   Em⁷   C²
Your grace is enough,   I'm covered in Your love

G   Dsus   C²   G
Your grace is enough   for me   for me

       Dsus   Em⁷   C²
(Spoken) For you,   for me   for us. Hey!

G   Dsus   C²   G

Look Like a Fool
MATT MAHER and BILL STAINES

KEY OF (B♭)

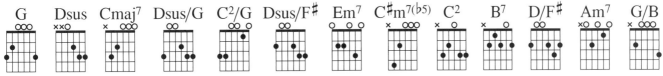

G   Dsus   Cmaj⁷   Dsus/G   C²/G   Dsus/F♯   Em⁷   C♯m⁷⁽♭⁵⁾   C²   B⁷   D/F♯   Am⁷   G/B

Capo 3rd fret (G)

G   Dsus   Cmaj⁷   G   Dsus   Cmaj⁷

VERSE 1:
G   Dsus/G   C²/G
All God's creatures got a place in the choir:
G   Dsus/G   C²/G
Some sing low and   some sing higher,
G   Dsus/F♯   Em⁷   Dsus
Some just hang out like a bird on a wire,
C♯m⁷⁽♭⁵⁾   Cmaj⁷
Wait - ing to fly home.
G   Dsus   C²
All God's children are the apple of His eye,
G   Dsus   C²
Even the ones   we can't stand sometimes;
G   Dsus/F♯   Em⁷
But we're coming togeth - er just to go outside,
Dsus   C♯m⁷⁽♭⁵⁾
And I need something to sing
Cmaj⁷
With this neigh - bor of mine.

CHORUS:
G   Em⁷   C²   Dsus
That's why grace is so amaz - ing,
G   Em⁷   C²   Dsus
That's why love is so absurd, and
G   Em⁷   C²   B⁷
That's why I sing for God unchang - ing;
C²   Dsus
That's why I don't care if I look like a fool.

G   Dsus   Cmaj⁷   G   Dsus   Cmaj⁷

CONTINUED...

VERSE 2:
G   Dsus/G   C²/G
All God's people got a reason to live;
G   Dsus/G   C²/G
Joy for the hard days, and true love to give.
G   Dsus/F♯   Em⁷
So we raise our hands, and lay down our sin,
Dsus   C♯m⁷⁽♭⁵⁾
And remem - ber the day
Cmaj⁷
Our free - dom began.

(REPEAT CHORUS 2x)

G   Dsus   Cmaj⁷

BRIDGE:
Em⁷   C♯m⁷⁽♭⁵⁾
Feed - ing the hungry, cloth - ing the naked,
Cmaj⁷   G   D/F♯
Giv - ing the homeless a place to rest;
Em⁷   C♯m⁷⁽♭⁵⁾
Vis - iting the prisoner, lift - ing up the lowly.
N.C.   Am⁷
By our fruits may You shine on us,
G/B
May You shine on us!
Cmaj⁷
Shine on us, Lord, shine on us.

(REPEAT CHORUS 2x)

G   Dsus   Cmaj⁷
If I look like a fool.
G   Dsus   Cmaj⁷   G

For Your Glory

MATT MAHER

KEY OF (E)

E   E^2(no^3)   Esus   A^2/C$^\sharp$ E/B   Bsus   A^2 C$^\sharp$m^7 E/G$^\sharp$ Amaj^9 B/D$^\sharp$ A^2(no^3)   F$^\sharp$m^7

E   E^2(no^3)   Esus   E

VERSE 1:

E   A^2/C$^\sharp$
   There is a time   to live,
E/B   Bsus
   There is a time   to die,
E   A^2
   There is a time   to laugh,
C$^\sharp$m^7 Bsus
   There is a time   to cry;
E   A^2
   There is a time   to dance,
E   Bsus
  A time for joy's   embrace;
E/G$^\sharp$ A^2
  And in all sea   -   sons, God,
C$^\sharp$m^7 Bsus
  We humbly seek   Your face.
Amaj^9 Bsus
   This is our of   -   fering to You,
A^2/C$^\sharp$ B/D$^\sharp$
   This is our of   -   fering.

CHORUS:

E
Everything I am is for Your glory,
A^2(no^3)   C$^\sharp$m^7 Bsus
Everything I am for You, a   -   lone;
E
Everything I am is for Your glory,
A^2(no^3)   C$^\sharp$m^7 Bsus
Everything I am for You, a   -   lone.

E   E^2(no^3)   Esus   E

CONTINUED...

VERSE 2:

E   A^2/C$^\sharp$
  There is a time   to sow,
E/B   Bsus
  There is a time   to reap,
E   A^2
  A time for vic   -   tory,
C$^\sharp$m^7 Bsus
  A time to claim   defeat;
E   A^2
  A time to be   renewed,
E   Bsus
  A time to be   reborn;
E/G$^\sharp$ A^2
  And in all sea   -   sons, God,
C$^\sharp$m^7 Bsus
  We bow before   Your throne.
Amaj^9 Bsus
   This is our of   -   fering to You,
A^2/C$^\sharp$ B/D$^\sharp$
   This is our of   -   fering.

(Repeat CHORUS)

CHORUS:

Amaj^9 Bsus   F$^\sharp$m^7 E/G$^\sharp$
  The earth stands   still with - out You,
  Amaj^9 Bsus   C$^\sharp$m^7
And we could only move because You made us to.
A^2(no^3)   Bsus   F$^\sharp$m^7 E
  The world is nothing with - out You,
  A^2(no^3)   Bsus   A^2/C$^\sharp$ B/D$^\sharp$
And we could only live because You made us to.
E   E^2(no^3)   Esus   E

E   E^2(no^3)   Esus   E

(Repeat CHORUS)

E

As It Is in Heaven

MATT MAHER and ED CASH

KEY OF (B)

G   D/F#   C²/E   C²   D   Dsus   Em   A⁷   Em⁷

[chord diagrams]

capo 4th fret (G)

G   D/F#   C²/E   C²   G   D   C²

VERSE 1:

      G   Dsus
Our Fath - er, Who art in Heav - en,
C²
Hallowed be Thy name.
Em   D
Come and let Your glory come,
            C²
And let Your glory fall.
      G   Dsus
Our Fath - er, Who art in Heav - en,
     C²
The rocks cry out Your name.
Em   D
Come and let Your glory come,
            C²
And let Your glory fall.

CHANNEL:

I will sing, sing a new song,
         A⁷
I will sing,   sing a new song;
       Em⁷   D   C²
I will sing,   sing a new   song to the Lord.

CHORUS:

             G
Let Your kingdom come,
         D
Let Your will be done
        Em⁷   C²
On earth,   as it is in Heav - en.

CHORUS CONTINUED...

             G
Every heart pro - claim
             D
The mercy of Your name,
        Em⁷   C²
On earth,   as it is in Heav - en.
G   D   C²

VERSE 2:

         G   Dsus
God give   us, new every morn - ing,
C²
Mercy as daily bread
Em
In the name of Jesus,
     D   C²
In   the name of Jesus we pray.
            G   Dsus
And lead   us not to tempta - tion,
          C²
But de - liver us with Your hand
Em
In the name of Jesus,
     D   C²
In   the name of Jesus we pray.   Father, we pray!

(Repeat CHANNEL and CHORUS)

BRIDGE:

              G   D
For the King - dom is Yours, and the pow - er is Yours,
          Em⁷   C²
And the glo - ry forever, amen.   ***(repeat 3x)***

(Repeat CHORUS 2x, 2nd x vocal ad-lib)

I Rejoice

MATT MAHER

KEY OF (D)

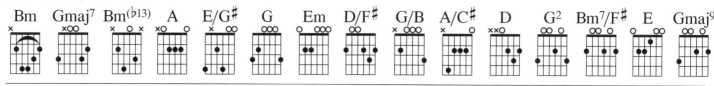

Bm   Gmaj⁷   Bm⁽ᵇ¹³⁾   A   E/G♯   G   Em   D/F♯   G/B   A/C♯   D   G²   Bm⁷/F♯   E   Gmaj⁹

CONTINUED...

Bm   Gmaj⁷   Bm   Gmaj⁷

VERSE 1:

Bm⁽ᵇ¹³⁾   Gmaj⁷   A
Underneath the shadow,
Bm⁽ᵇ¹³⁾   Gmaj⁷   A
Underneath the shadow,
Bm⁽ᵇ¹³⁾   Gmaj⁷   A
Underneath the shadow of Your wings,
     E/G♯   G
Lord and King, You cover   me.

CHANNEL:

Em D/F♯   G A G A G/B A/C♯
I re - joice,   I re - joice, I re - joice. I re - joice

CHORUS:

  D A/C♯   Bm   G
In You, in You; I re - joice in You.
  D A/C♯   Bm   G
In You, in You; I re - joice in You.

Bm   G   Bm   G

VERSE 2:

Bm⁽ᵇ¹³⁾   Gmaj⁷   A
Underneath the shadow,
Bm⁽ᵇ¹³⁾   Gmaj⁷   A
Underneath the shadow,
Bm⁽ᵇ¹³⁾   Gmaj⁷   A
Underneath the shadow of the cross,
     E/G♯   G
You bore the cost, and death has   lost.

(Repeat CHANNEL and CHORUS)

BRIDGE:

Bm   G²
    With arms spread out like eagle's wings
Bm   G²   A
    As love lays out a wedding feast—
Bm⁷/F♯
    Your body and Your blood.
G²
    And now we have become
E   D/F♯   G   A
    Your sons and Your daught - ers:

(Repeat CHORUS)

Bm   G   Bm   Gmaj⁹

Maranatha (Come Again)
MATT MAHER

KEY OF (G)

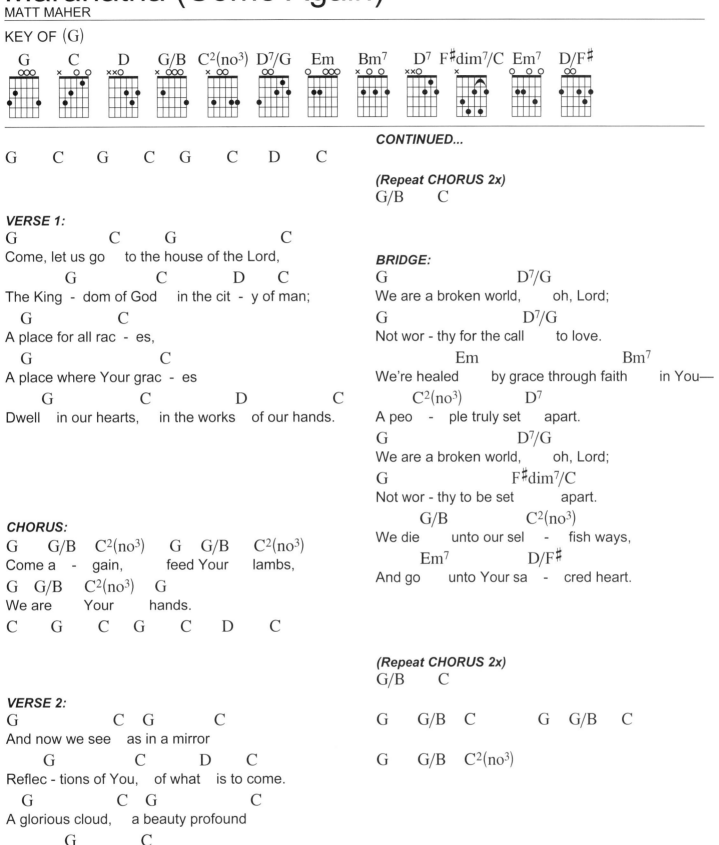

G   C   G   C   G   C   D   C

CONTINUED...

(Repeat CHORUS 2x)
G/B   C

VERSE 1:
G   C   G   C
Come, let us go   to the house of the Lord,
           G   C   D   C
The King - dom of God   in the cit - y of man;
  G   C
A place for all rac - es,
  G   C
A place where Your grac - es
      G   C   D   C
Dwell   in our hearts,   in the works   of our hands.

BRIDGE:
G D^7/G
We are a broken world,   oh, Lord;
G D^7/G
Not wor - thy for the call   to love.
              Em Bm^7
We're healed   by grace through faith   in You—
     $C^2(no^3)$ D^7
A peo - ple truly set   apart.
G D^7/G
We are a broken world,   oh, Lord;
G $F^\#dim^7$/C
Not wor - thy to be set   apart.
        G/B $C^2(no^3)$
We die   unto our sel   -   fish ways,
       Em^7 D/F$^\#$
And go   unto Your sa - cred heart.

CHORUS:
G   G/B $C^2(no^3)$ G G/B $C^2(no^3)$
Come a -   gain,   feed Your   lambs,
G G/B $C^2(no^3)$ G
We are   Your   hands.
C   G   C   G   C   D   C

(Repeat CHORUS 2x)
G/B   C

G   G/B   C   G   G/B   C

G   G/B $C^2(no^3)$

VERSE 2:
G   C G   C
And now we see   as in a mirror
      G   C   D   C
Reflec - tions of You,   of what   is to come.
  G   C G   C
A glorious cloud,   a beauty profound
      G   C
In the wid - ow, the or - phan,
        D   C
The lame,   and the poor.

Great Things

MATT MAHER

KEY OF (G)

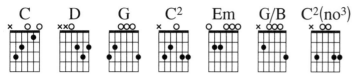

C   D   G   C   D   G

(repeat)

VERSE:

    C   D   G C^2 Em   D
My soul pro - clams Your great - ness, Lord,

    C   D   G   G/B C^2
Re - joic - ing in   my Sav - ior.

    C   D   G C^2 Em   D
Your mer - cy be - longs to those who fear Your Son;

    C   D   G   G/B C^2
His blessing You have given them forev - er.

CHANNEL:

    G/B C^2 D
And Holy   is His name,
G/B C^2 G/B   D
Holy   is   His   name.

CHORUS:

    G
You alone have done great things,
    D
I can't boast of anything;
    C   G   Em   D
Mighty One, and King of kings,   Jesus.
$C^2(no^3)$ G
You alone have done great things
    D
By Your living word in me;
    C   G   Em   D
Mighty One, and King of kings,   Jesus.

CONTINUED...

Em   C   D   G   C   D   G

(REPEAT VERSE, CHANNEL, and CHORUS)

BRIDGE:

    $C^2(no^3)$ G
And it's Your name we're shouting out,
D   Em
Shouting out loud.
    $C^2(no^3)$ G
It's Your name we're shouting out,
D
Shouting out loud.   **(repeat 3x)**

(REPEAT CHORUS)

    G
Well, it's Your name we're shouting out,

Shouting out loud.
    D
It's Your name we're shouting out,

Shouting out loud.
    C
It's Your name we're shouting out,

Shouting out loud.
    D
It's Your name we're shouting out, shouting out.
    G

Leave a Light On

MATT MAHER

KEY OF (C)

C   Am   Fmaj⁷   F⁶⁄₉   F²   F²/C   Fmaj⁹   Dm⁷   G   F/A   F   Dm⁹   G⁷   Em⁷   Cmaj⁷   Em   C⁷/B♭   Fm/A♭

C   Am   C   Fmaj⁷   C   Am   C

VERSE 1:

F⁶⁄₉   C   F²   C
Where did You go?

   F²/C   C   F²   C
Jesus, where did You go?

          Fmaj⁹
You flew into the clouds,   we worship and we doubt;

       Dm⁷
Now I'm leap - ing for joy and sinking.

               C   F²   C
And where are You now?

   F²/C   C   F²   C
Jesus, where are You now?

          Fmaj⁹
Hidden in the skies   behind the poor man's eyes,

       Dm⁷
In our wait - ing and our serving

CHANNEL:

               G
Until You take us home,

         F/A   F
Until You return.

CHORUS:

           C   F
I'll leave a light on   for You, my Lord,

           C   F
I'll leave a light on   for You, my Lord,

        Am   F
Your Spirit inside,   burning bright—

I'll leave a light on.
C   Am   C   F   C   Am   C

CONTINUED...

VERSE 1:

F⁶⁄₉   C   F²   C
Here You are found,

        F²/C   C   F²   C
Jesus, here You are found—

                 Fmaj⁹
In the breaking of the bread,   the waking of the dead,

         Dm⁷
In our dy - ing and our rising

(Repeat CHANNEL and CHORUS)

C   Fmaj⁹

BRIDGE:
Dm⁹   F   G⁷   Em⁷

Am   Dm⁹
  Give me oil in my lamp;

G⁷   Cmaj⁷
  Keep it burning 'til the break of day.

F   Dm⁷
  Give me oil in my lamp;

Em   G⁷   C
  Keep it burning 'til the break of day.

          C⁷/B♭   F/A
Give me oil in my lamp, give me oil in my lamp;

            Fm/A♭
Keep me burning 'til the break of day.

C   Fmaj⁷   Am   F²

(Repeat CHORUS 2x)

C   Fmaj⁷   C   Fmaj⁷
           Shine on through the dark - ness.

Am   Fmaj⁷   C
    Shine on, shine on.

Shine Like the Son

MATT MAHER

KEY OF (D)

D   G   C   Bm   A   A/C#   D/F#   Asus

D   G   C   D   G   C

VERSE 1:

D   G
   How beauti - ful
         D   G
Are the hands and feet of those
         D   G
Bringing the good news to all the world,
         D   G   C   D
Bringing the good news to all the world.
         G
And how beauti - ful,
         D   G
The sound of all Your people in love
         D   G
With Someone so much greater than them - selves,
         D   G
Someone so much greater than them - selves.

CHANNEL:

     Bm   A   G
You've made us   ready.
    (Bm   A/C#   G)
(You've made us   worthy.)   **(2nd x only)**

CHORUS:

D   G   D   G
Shine like the Son,   shine like the Son.
D or Bm   G or E   G
Shine like the Son,   for everyone,
       A
For everyone,   for everyone!

CONTINUED...

VERSE 2:

D   G
   How beauti - ful
         D   G
Are the hands and feet of those
         D   G
Working in the vineyard of the Lord,
         D   G   C   D
Working in the vineyard of the Lord.
         G
And blessed are those
         D   G
Going in the name of the Lord,
         D   G
In the middle of the lost and the poor,
         D   G
We're living in the name of the Lord.

(Repeat CHANNEL and CHORUS)

BRIDGE:

Bm   D
    Announcing peace, as the prodigals come home;
       G   D/F#
And You open up the doors,
       G   Asus
And the prodigals come home.
Bm   A   G   D/F#
   Setting the captives free by Your word.
       G   D/F#
And You free us by Your word,
       G   Asus
You free us by Your word.

(Repeat CHORUS 2x)

D   G   C   D   G   C   D

Unwavering

MATT MAHER

KEY OF (E♭)

C   F6/A   Fmaj13/A   F/C   Dm9   C/G   G   F6/C   C/E   F2   Gsus   Am7   G/B   F   F/A   G(add4)   Fmaj9

Capo 3rd fret (C)

C   F6/A   C

VERSE 1:

                  F6/A   C
Blessed are the poor—the kingdom is theirs,
        Fmaj13/A   F/C   Dm9
Alive in the promise to be dead to the world.
           C   F6/A   C
Blessed are the meek in awe of You, Father;
    F6/A   C/G   G   C   F6/C
The Word at Your right hand,   the Spirit of truth.

CHORUS:

C   C/E   F2   C
  Un - wavering is Your voice,
         Gsus   G   C
Un - wavering is   Your hand;
         Am7   G/B   C
Un - wavering is   the   heart
   Am7   Gsus
That bled for the sins of man.
G   C/E   F2   C
  Un - wavering is Your will,
        Gsus   G   Am7
Un - wavering is   Your plan;
   C/E   Gsus
The fount of sal - vation
G   (C   F   C)
  On which we will stand.   **(last time Am7)**

VERSE 2:

               F/A   C
Blessed are the righteous on bended knee,
F/A   Fmaj13/A   Dm9
Bound in this freedom, committed to You.

VERSE 2 CONTINUED...

          C   F/A   C
Blessed are those who see the heights of glory
F6/A   C/G G   C F/C
Found in the valley,   in suffering for You.

(Repeat CHORUS)

BRIDGE:

      C/E   F2   Am7   G(add4)
Send us out to   be Your hands and feet.
                       (repeat 2x)

(Repeat CHORUS)

F2   C/G
  The fount of sal - vation
G   Fmaj9   Am7   G
  On which we will stand.
Fmaj9   Am7   G

      C/E   Fmaj9 Am7   Gsus
Send us out to   be Your hands and feet.
      C/E   Fmaj9 Am7   Gsus
Send us out to   be Your hands and feet.
      C/E   Fmaj9 F2/A   Gsus/B
Send us out to   be Your hands and feet.
      C/E   Fmaj9 F2/A   G(add4)
Send us out to   be Your hands and   feet.
      C/E   F2   Am7   G(add4)
Send us out to   be Your hands and feet.
      C/E   F2   Am7   G(add4)
Send us out to   be Your hands and   feet.
C/E   F2   Gsus   C

Lay It Down

MATT MAHER and BRENTON BROWN

KEY OF (D♭)

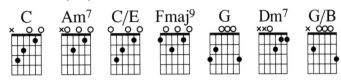

C   Am⁷   C/E   Fmaj⁹   G   Dm⁷   G/B

Capo 1st fret (C)

C   Am⁷   C/E   Fmaj⁹   Am⁷   G

VERSE:

C   Am⁷
   Everything I am,   everything I long to be—
C/E   Fmaj⁹ Am⁷   G
   I lay it down   at   Your feet.
C
   Everything I am,   everything I long to be—
C/E   Fmaj⁹ Am⁷   G
   I lay it down   at   Your feet.

CHORUS:

C   C/E
   I lay it down,   I lay it down,
Fmaj⁹   Am⁷ G
   I lay it down   at Your feet.
C   C/E
   I lay it down,   I lay it down,
Fmaj⁹   Am⁷ (G   Fmaj⁹)
   I lay it down   (at Your feet.) *(omit 2nd x)*

(Repeat VERSE and CHORUS)

CONTINUED...

BRIDGE (repeat once):

G   Fmaj⁹
Oh, pearl of great   -   est price,
              C/E
No act of sac - rifice
                Dm⁷
Can match the gift   of life
G/B   C
   I find within Your gaze.
            Fmaj⁹
Oh, what a sweet   exchange:
         C/E
I die to rise   again,
         Dm⁷
Lifted up from   the grave
(*G   C)   **(*1st x only)**
  *(Into Your hands of grace.)

G/B   Am⁷   C/E   Fmaj⁹
   Into Your hands of   grace.

CHORUS:

C   C/E
   I lay it down,   I lay it down,
Fmaj⁹   Am⁷ G/B
   I lay it down   at   Your feet. **(repeat 2**
C   C/E
   I lay it down,   I lay it down,
Fmaj⁹   Am⁷ G   C
   I lay it down   at   Your feet.

Empty and Beautiful

MATT MAHER

KEY OF (A♭)

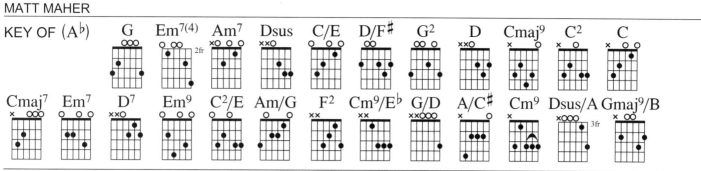

Capo 1st fret (G)

(Piano intro)

VERSE 1:
G   Em⁷⁽⁴⁾
   My past won't stop haunting me.
   Am⁷
In this prison there's a fight between
Dsus   C/E   D/F♯
Who I am, and who I used   to be.
G²   Em⁷⁽⁴⁾
   This thorn in my side is a grace,
   Am⁷   D
For be - cause of it, the flesh and blood of God
                Cmaj⁹
Was offered in my place,   my place.

CHORUS: (chords may vary slightly on repeats)
   G²   C²   Dsus   D
You fought the fight   in me,
   G   C   Am⁷
You chased me down   and fin - ished the race.
Dsus   D   G   C²   Dsus
     I was blind, but now   I see;
D   Cmaj⁷   Dsus
Jesus, You kept   the faith   in me.
(G   Em⁷   C²   D⁷)   **(1st x only)**

VERSE 1:
G   Em⁹
   Where did my best friends go?
   Am⁷
At my   defense they disappeared,
   Dsus   C/E   D/F♯
Just like Your friends did to You,   oh Lord.
G²   Em⁷⁽⁴⁾
   But You were there, You gave me strength,
   Am⁷   Dsus
So this little one might come to know
          C²/E   Cmaj⁹
The glory of Your name,   Your name.

CONTINUED...

(Repeat CHORUS)
G   Am/G   G²

VERSE 4:
   F²
I'm wait - ing, and set apart,
      C²/E
Like in - cense to Your heart—
      Cm⁹/E♭
A liba - tion I'm pouring out,
          G/D
Empty and beau - tiful,
    A/C♯   Cm⁹
Beau - tiful, beau - tiful.

(Repeat CHORUS)
C²

(Repeat CHORUS)
Gmaj⁹/B

                C²   D   Gmaj⁹/B
Jesus, You kept   the faith   in me.
                C²   Dsus
Savior, You kept   the faith   in me.

G   Em   C   D⁷

G   Em   C   D⁷   G

Over two thousand years, men and women have responded to God's invitation to grace, all as part of the Body of Christ; the church. To accept the revelation that Jesus Christ is Lord and Savior of mankind; that He paid the price for all of humanity's transgressions, and that this gift of reconciliation with God is made for all to receive freely through the cross. As part of the body, each person's response is lived in a way as unique as the individual. Yet, despite the distance of time, culture, and ethnic origins, each call is connected in common struggles and themes, chief of which is, as Jesus says in the gospel of Luke, to "pick up his cross and follow me".... to empty oneself and be filled with that beautiful grace. To be 'empty and beautiful.'

For singer/songwriter/worship leader Matt Maher, there is nothing more special about his call than any-one else's, and like those before him, he is trying to live that same call, as his 12-track Essential Records debut album's title says, to be made Empty & Beautiful. Maher breaks open these two simple words on the project, in songs that are both corporate and reflective; driving and soft; each one telling the story from a different perspective. Empty & Beautiful was co-produced by Maher and Jeff Thomas, except for, "As It Is In Heaven," which was produced by Ed Cash (Chris Tomlin, Bebo Norman, Bethany Dillon).

Born and raised in Newfoundland, Canada, Matt grew up in a strong culture comprised of two elements: music and tradition. "Music is part of the fabric of the culture there, similar to places like Louisiana or the Appalachian mountains; and over the years, not just Celtic music, but music of every kind. "I grew up listening to American Top 40 with Casey Kasem every Saturday, rain or shine. My dad would cook while listening to Willie Nelson or Frank Sinatra. My cousins, who lived next door, listened to everything from Broadway to British Rock, like the Beatles and The Who." Early in life, Matt's parents realized his talent for music and started him in piano lessons. He quickly absorbed as many musical styles as possible, playing in concert and jazz ensembles, singing in choir, and even playing in a high school garage rock band.

Matt's collegiate years began while he was still in Newfoundland. At this time, life lessons abounded, and most of them were difficult ones. In 1995, Matt's parents divorced. His mother, an American citizen, decided to move back to the United States to be closer to her family. After careful consideration, Matt decided to move with his mom. "I remember realizing in my heart that I was going nowhere, and quickly. I had made some poor decisions during college. I was a very sensitive soul. During those years, it's easy for people and life to break your heart. I knew I needed a new start, so I moved to Arizona with dreams of becoming a film-scorer." Matt assumed a brief stay in Arizona would help him adjust to American life, but God had different plans.

"I had been raised believing in God, but music was my religion in a way. Once high school came, I stopped going to church. I would pray at night before I went to bed. I had a Bible in my room and would read Genesis and Revelation, because I was fascinated with how we got here, and how we're going out, but that was all. My relationship with God was not very strong. I knew He was real, I just didn't know how much He loved me."

Matt started attending church with his cousin and her friends, looking for deeper answers and friendship. This is where he witnessed a church youth group for the first time. What Matt found was something more than friends—he found Jesus Christ.

While attending his new church in Arizona, Matt was approached by the youth pastor and the music director to help out. "They both saw something in me that I didn't see, and I know it was God leading me closer to Him. Within two months, I was led to accept what Christ did for me on the cross, and to respond in serving Him in my new church community." During this time, Matt restarted work on his music degree and received a scholarship from the Jazz Department at Arizona State University, where he studied Jazz Piano.

After a few years, Matt was led to another community, St. Timothy Catholic Community in Mesa, Arizona, where he has been since. While being mentored by Dove Award-nominated songwriter and artist Tom Booth ("I Will Choose Christ," "Nothing Is Beyond You"), Matt met and worked with several artists along the way, including Israel Houghton, Kathy Troccoli, and Rich Mullins, whom Maher credits with helping him land his job at St. Tim's.

Matt shares, "Rich and Tom were friends, and Rich wanted to do a performance of his musical "Canticle of The Plains" at St Tim's. Rich asked Tom to cast it. Tom called me and asked me if was interested. I said, 'Uhh, sure,' at that point having no idea who Rich was. This was a major turning point for me. I couldn't get over this guy; he was so real, yet he loved God so much, but without all the superficial piety." Matt's character, Ivory, was a piano player who made his living playing at a hotel saloon, a job Maher knew well. He paid for his first three years of college by playing piano in a hotel in his hometown. This series of events, like many others to follow, helped deepen Matt's commitment to Christ. A few years later, another movement became more present - modern worship music.

"I was in my last year of college, unsure of what to do next, when I heard the songs of Delirious? and song-writers like Paul Baloche and Darrell Evans, as well as the Passion movement. This stuff blew me away. It was in those simple expressions that I realized my desire to do the same thing." Maher took a full time position at St Tim's, and started writing songs for his church.

Ten years and many songs later, Maher is now travelling full time as a "musical missionary," and is still involved in local church ministry at St Timothy Catholic Community, as well as helping out with the young adult ministry at All Saints Newman Center, on the campus of Arizona State University. "You have to stay rooted in community if you want to lead and write for the Church. That is where your songs come from – from your relationship with Christ, with your immediate family, and the family of believers."

Besides serving with organizations like WorshipTogether.com, SpiritandSong.com, Passion, Youth Specialties, and Adore Ministries, Matt is a contributing artist for Life Teen, a high school youth movement that helped lead him to Jesus; his songs are being sung by the church around the world. A number of Matt Maher-written songs have been recorded by other artists, including: "Your Grace is Enough," a song for the church originally recorded by Maher's good friend, Chris Tomlin; "Unwavering," a reflection on the Beatitudes (recorded prior by Bethany Dillon); "For Your Glory," a new testament response to the book of Ecclesiastes (recorded by Phillips, Craig and Dean). Other songs include "As It Is In Heaven," a song based on the Lord's Prayer, originally written by Matt, now re-worked with acclaimed producer Ed Cash; and "Great Things," a look at the song of Mary, the Magnificat. "I'm always looking in for biblical songs for the church, and here you have this amazing prayer song by the first human being to accept Jesus Christ into her being; a 14-year old girl who literally carried God in her womb. Amazing."

Matt continues, sharing his inspiration behind the song "Empty & Beautiful." "'Hold fast to the confessions you have received,' Paul says to Timothy. When you read all of Paul's letters, you see the transformation of a man into a follower of Christ: 'I've kept the faith. I've fought the fight. I've finished the race.' You see the truth of God, despite the reality of Paul's humanness. It's the miracle of grace being revealed," as the chorus to the title track illustrates:

> You fought the fight in me / You chased me down and finished the race / I was blind but now I see / Jesus, You kept the faith in me

"In life, we end up having to empty ourselves to achieve that which is beautiful," Matt says. "If you don't, you never really get made beautiful. It's a weird dichotomy, especially in the world we live in because there's so much focus on beauty. The whole idea of having to empty one's self to achieve beauty is completely counter cultural, but that's what happens—marriage, service of the poor, sharing the beauty of the gospel. That's what Christ calls us to do, and I hope these songs will help inspire people to follow Jesus in that way."

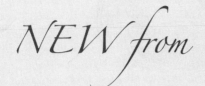